AFRICA FOCUS

AFRICAN CULTURE

Rob Bowden and Rosie Wilson

Heinemann LIBRARY

www.heinemannlibrary.co.uk
Visit our website to find out more information about Heinemann Library books.

To order:

☎ Phone +44 (0) 1865 888066

🖷 Fax +44 (0) 1865 314091

🖳 Visit www.heinemannlibrary.co.uk

Edited by Louise Galpine and Rachel Howells
Designed by Richard Parker and Manhattan Design
Original illustrations © 2008
Illustrated by Oxford Designers and Illustrators and International Mapping (p.14)
Picture research by Mica Brancic
Originated by Heinemann Library
Printed in China by Leo Paper Products Ltd.

ISBN 978-0431020785 (hardback)
13 12 11 10 09
10 9 8 7 6 5 4 3 2 1

British Library Cataloguing in Publication Data
Bowden, Rob
African Culture. - (Africa focus)
I. Title II. Wilson, Rosalind
960
A full catalogue record for this book is available from the British Library.

Acknowledgements

We would like to thank the following for permission to reproduce photographs: Alamy p. **40** (© Vehbi Koca); Corbis pp. **8** (© Ed Kashi), **9** (© Nic Bothma/ epa), **11** (© Bob Krist) **15** (© Gideon Mendel), **30** (© Lynn Goldsmith), **34** (© Penny Tweedie); EASI-Images p. **41** (Neil Thomson); Eye Ubiquitous p. **13** (Hutchison); Getty Images pp. **18** (Lonely Planet Images/ Craig Pershouse), **19** (Stuart Price/ Stringer/AFP), **20** (© Per-Anders Pettersson), **25** (Gallo Images/ Martin Harvey), **28** (AFP/ Stringer), **36** (Stone/ Jason Dewey), **39** (© David Levenson); Photolibrary pp. **7** (Oxford Scientific/ © Ariadne Van Zandbergen), **10** (Imagestate/ © Alan Keohane), **16** (Photographer's Choice/ Sylvester Adams), **22** (Paul Nevin), **23** (John Warburton-Lee Photography/ Mark Hannaford), **26** (Japan Travel Bureau/ Haga Library), **29** (Robert Harding Travel/ Peter Groenendijk), **33** (Imagestate/ David South).

Cover photograph of women performing a traditional dance in Ethiopia's Ogaden region, reproduced with permission of Reuters (Barry Malone).

We would like to thank Danny Block for his invaluable help in the preparation of this book.

Every effort has been made to contact copyright holders of material reproduced in this book. Any omissions will be rectified in subsequent printings if notice is given to the publishers.

All the Internet addresses (URLs) given in this book were valid at the time of going to press. However, due to the dynamic nature of the Internet, some addresses may have changed, or sites may have changed or ceased to exist since publication. While the author and Publishers regret any inconvenience this may cause readers, no responsibility for any such changes can be accepted by either the author or the Publishers.

Contents

Introduction to Africa 4

African traditions... 6

Peoples and languages.. 10

Family and daily life 16

Religion, beliefs, and customs.. 24

Performing arts 30

Visual arts 34

Africa and global culture 38

Timeline 42

Glossary... 44

Find out more.. 46

Index.. 48

Some words are printed in bold, **like this**. You can find out what they mean by looking in the glossary on page 44.

Introduction to Africa

Africa is the world's second largest **continent** and has 53 individual countries. It is so large that you could fit the United States, China, and India into it and still have room for all 27 countries of the **European Union (EU)**!

African culture

Africa's landscapes include deserts, forests, mountains, lakes, coasts, and rivers. Its peoples are just as varied. African **culture** grew from the ways in which Africa's people relate to their landscapes and to one another. It is about how people live, and what they do and enjoy. African traditions, behaviour, language, dress, food, music, and art are all parts of African culture. With so many different peoples and landscapes, African culture is extremely varied.

Cultural changes

African cultures have long spread their influence to other parts of the world. This happened especially between the 1300s and 1800s, when thousands of African **slaves** were sent to the Americas and took their cultures with them. But earlier **trade** and **immigration** also brought African culture to different regions.

African cultures have also been influenced by people from outside of Africa for thousands of years. **Islam**, for example, came to North Africa with traders from the Middle East. During the 1800s and 1900s, European **colonization** of Africa had a major impact on African culture. European languages were introduced and new land boundaries divided traditional cultural groups.

Twenty-first century Africa

Today Africa is changing again. Technology such as television, greater travel, and the Internet is allowing African cultures to mix with other cultures more easily. This is creating exciting new chapters in the story of Africa's long and fascinating culture.

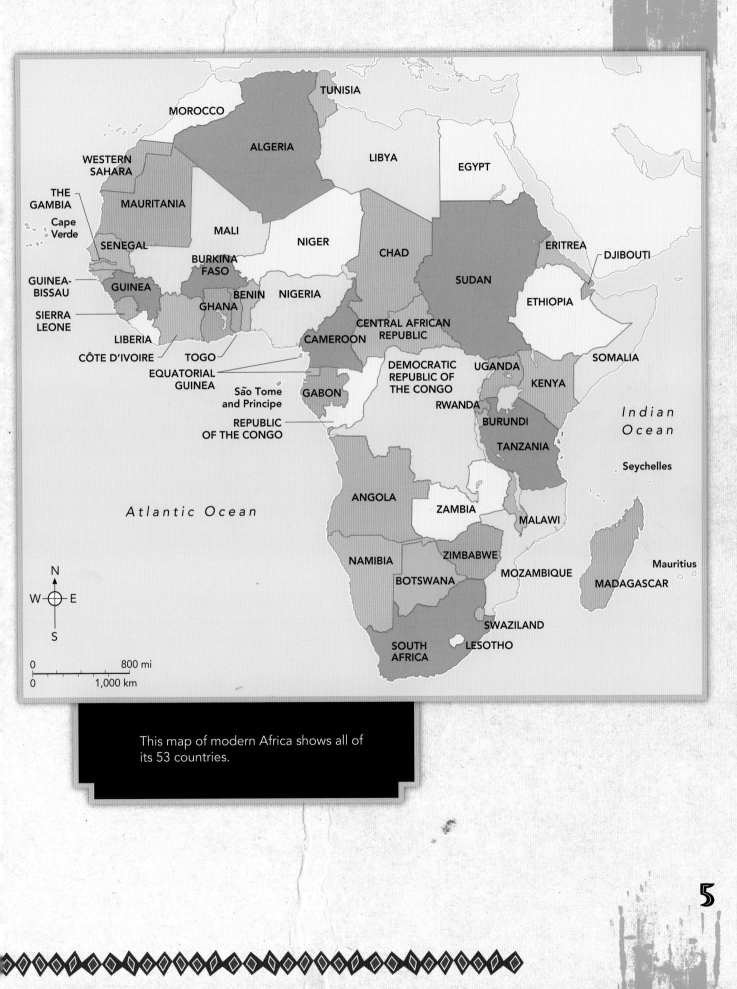

This map of modern Africa shows all of its 53 countries.

African traditions

The first humans are thought to have come from Africa and then spread slowly around the world. In much of the world, the ancient traditions of these early humans are long lost. But they can still be found in some parts of Africa, despite thousands of years of change. The Kalahari San of Botswana and Namibia, for example, lead a hunting and gathering lifestyle that **archaeologists** believe is very similar to that of the first humans.

AFRICA FACT

Human bones dating back around 1.2 million years show that the first humans probably came from Africa. The bones were discovered at Olduvai gorge in Tanzania and Lake Turkana in Kenya.

Kalahari San

Ancient rock paintings in southern Africa show us that the San have lived in the Kalahari Desert for at least 10,000 years. Many of their ways of living have changed little, such as being able to move easily by staying in small family groups and having few possessions. Their lack of possessions means the San are very creative. They use their hunting bows as musical instruments, for example. Sounds are made by playing the bow string with the mouth or against a hollow container.

Ancient societies

Some of the world's oldest known societies (groups of people) are African. The remains of artwork and jewellery found in southern Africa are signs that there were organized societies there up to 100,000 years ago. Rock paintings found in the Sahara Desert show that people had begun to farm **crops** and animals by around 9000 BCE. These early forms of farming were the secret to the success of Africa's most famous early society, the Ancient Egyptians. They lived in the Nile Valley of Egypt in around 3100–1200 BCE.

The San of the Kalahari Desert in southern Africa hunt with a bow and arrow. Their lifestyle and culture are thought to be similar to that of the very earliest humans.

Villagers in the Niger Delta celebrate a local harvest festival called "Funfu Ma Tie", which dates back to the 16th century.

Harvest festivals

Most people in Africa worked in farming. Because of this, many festivals and **customs** are about celebrating a good **harvest**. Yams (a potato-like crop) are the main food of the Igbo people in Nigeria. Each year in August they celebrate the yam harvest with a festival called *Iwa-ji*, meaning "new yam". **Rituals** are performed to thank God and the **ancestors** for a good harvest. The community gather to celebrate with music, dancing, and of course, to taste the new yams!

Naming ceremonies

Names are important in Africa. They can tell others where you are from, what was happening when you were born, whether you are a twin, or even on what day you were born. In Ghana, the Akan people give their children one name based upon the day of the week they were born. Each week day has different male or female names. The main names are shown in the table below.

Day of the week	Male name	Female name
Sunday	Kwesi, Kwasi, Akwesi	Akosua, Akousia, Esi
Monday	Kwodwo, Kwadwo, Kojo	Adwoa, Adjoa
Tuesday	Kobena , Kwabena	Abenaa
Wednesday	Kweku, Kwaku, Ako	Ekua, Akua, Aquia, Akwia
Thursday	Yaw, Yao, Yawu, Kwaw, Kwao	Yaa, Aba
Friday	Kofi, Kwafi	Efua, Afua, Afia
Saturday	Kwame, Kwamena	Ama, Amma, Amba, Ame

AFRICA FACT

Akan birthday names are also called "soul names" and describe what type of person you are supposed to be. According to tradition, you are calm and peaceful if born on a Monday and a wanderer or traveller if born on a Friday.

Old and new

Modern life in Africa is very different from the past, but traditions are still strong. When people fall ill they may visit a local healer instead of a modern doctor, for example. People starting a new business may still make **offerings** to the ancestors in the belief it will bring them good fortune. Tradition has also survived in clothing styles. Even modern clothing often uses traditional patterns, shapes, and colours.

A model wears an outfit by the designer Akinka from Burundi during Cape Town fashion week. Modern African fashion is often an exciting mix of the old and new.

Peoples and languages

African people

A group of people who share the same background are known as an **ethnic group**. They will normally have similar physical characteristics, share the same **customs**, and speak the same language. Africa has hundreds of ethnic groups and at least 1,500 spoken languages.

In the past, ethnic groups in Africa were often limited to very particular areas, but over hundreds of years people have moved and ethnic groups have become mixed up. In parts of Uganda, for example, it is possible to find over 15 different ethnic groups living in a single village.

North African Berbers

The Berbers mainly live in the deserts and mountains of North Africa and farm **livestock**. They live in groups called **clans**, which are made up of several related families. The clans also group together to form communities with an elected leader or chieftain.

Some Berber communities are **nomadic**. This means they move from place to place to find food and water for themselves and their livestock. Other Berbers have land on the edge of the desert where they grow **crops** during the winter. In the hot summers they leave their fields and live in the cooler mountains with their livestock.

Berber herdsmen trade sheep and goats at a market in Imilchil, Morocco.

Dogon tribesmen wear traditional costumes and masks during a festival in Bamako, Mali.

The Dogon of Mali

The Dogon live in the mountains and central **plateau** of Mali, in West Africa. Most of them are farmers, but some are highly-skilled craftsmen. The Dogon have a spiritual leader called a "hogon" who is an important symbol of Dogon beliefs. These beliefs are based on their knowledge of the stars.

Maasai Warriors

The Maasai live in Kenya and Tanzania. They are traditionally nomadic people who survive on the meat, blood, and milk of their cattle. They live in clans that are ruled by men and organized by age. When a boy reaches 14 years, he takes part in a ceremony to become a "moran", or **warrior**. He then spends up to 15 years living away from his family in the African **bush** with other morani. He will train to be strong and fearless and learn tribal customs. Later, he will become a senior warrior, junior elder, and then senior elder. Only senior elders can make decisions for the whole clan.

Rise of the Zulu

The Zulu live in highly organized societies in South Africa. Families live in clans that are ruled by the oldest Zulu man in the clan. The Zulu are famous warriors. They were once led by the fearsome Shaka (around 1787–1828). Shaka led his armies to attack neighbouring clans and tribes and made the Zulu into the largest ethnic group in South Africa. It is said that over two million people were killed by Shaka and his warriors. The Zulu now live peacefully with other people in South Africa, but still have great pride in their past. They have kept traditions such as their strictly organized society.

Madagascar

Madagascar is a large island off the southeast coast of Africa. The Madagascan people have close cultural links with Southeast Asia and do not consider themselves to be African. Their language, called Malagasy, is related to languages from Indonesia, for example (these languages are known as Austronesian – see the map on page 14). The island and its people have been treated as part of Africa since they were **colonized** by France between 1896 and 1958. French is still a national language in Madagascar today.

These men are morani (young warriors) of the Maasai tribe. They are preparing for a ceremony that boys go through to become men.

Languages

Africa has more than 1,500 languages, with over 300 spoken in Nigeria alone! When languages are different but share some features, they are part of a **language family**. In addition to the Austronesian languages, Africa has four main language families.

- In North Africa people speak Afro-Asiatic languages. These include Arabic, Berber, and Hausa.

- South of the Sahara Desert most Africans speak Niger-Congo languages. There are around 1,400 of these languages, including Zulu, Mande, and Kikuyu.

- Where these northern and southern language families meet there is a group of languages called the Nilo-Saharan languages. The Maasai and Turkana are examples of people who speak these languages.

- The last language family is the Khoisan languages of southern Africa, which are known for their use of "clicks". They are spoken by people such as the San of the Kalahari Desert.

Key
- Afro-Asiatic
- Nilo-Saharan
- Niger-Congo
- Khoisan
- Austronesian

Mediterranean Sea

Atlantic Ocean

Indian Ocean

N
W   E
S

0   500   1,000 mi
0   500   1,000 km

This map shows the main language families of Africa. Experts are still working out exactly how many languages there are within these bigger groups.

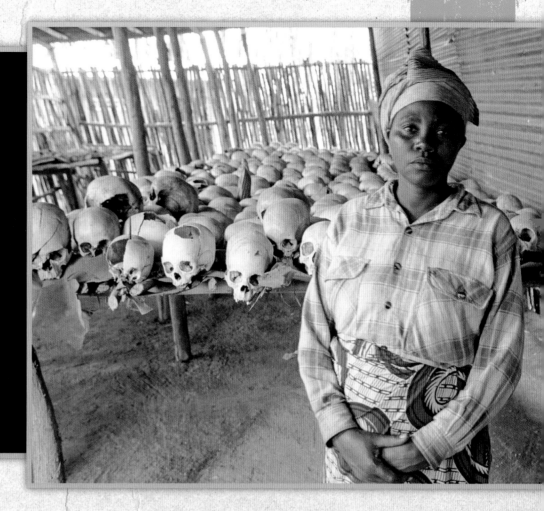

A woman stands in front of human skulls at Ntamara Church in Kigali, Rwanda. Around one million people were killed when Hutu and Tutsi tribal groups began to fight for control of Rwanda in 1994. The two tribes are very similar. They speak the same language, live in the same areas, and follow the same traditions. However, Belgian colonists thought the Tutsis were superior to the Hutus, and this is how the trouble began.

Common voices

To help communication between Africa's many different people, Africa has adopted several common languages. These are sometimes people's first language, but are more often used as a second language that allows people to communicate more easily.

- The most commonly spoken language in Africa is Arabic. It is especially important in North Africa and helps the region to have strong **trade** and cultural links with Arabic-speaking countries in the Middle East.

- English is the most widespread language in Africa. It arrived with English-speaking **missionaries** and spread during the **colonial** period. French was also introduced as a common colonial language and is still widely used across West Africa.

- Swahili is an African common language that began on Zanzibar and the East African coast. Nowadays it is a common trade and **cultural** language across East Africa. Fulani is another common African language and is widely used in West Africa.

Family and daily life

Daily life in Africa is extremely varied. People living in **rural** areas may have a very different life from those living in Africa's cities. Despite such differences, some parts of daily life are similar across the **continent**. It is most often men that are the head of communities and families, for example. The family unit is of great importance to African life and can be very large.

Changing family life

In the past, many African families lived close to each other in the same village or area, but this way of life is now less common. One reason for this is that more people are leaving rural areas to live in towns and cities. This is called **urbanization**. It is harder for families to live together in **urban** housing, which is normally more crowded and expensive than in rural areas. Almost 40 per cent of all Africans were already living in a town or city by 2007, and the number was increasing by around 1,500 people every hour!

Traditional clothing such as these loose flowing cotton robes are well suited to the climate in Cameroon. They remain popular even when western style clothes are easily available.

Elders

Older people are treated with great respect in African **culture** and are commonly known as Elders. They are often selected as political or social leaders because of their greater knowledge of life. Some people become Elders based on power and wealth, and some are elected to be Elders after people vote for them. In societies such as the Zulu or Maasai, a man becomes an Elder automatically once he reaches a certain age.

Elders play an important part in preserving African societies. Traditionally, Elders were responsible for using spoken words to pass down the knowledge, history, and culture of their people. It is only quite recently that these things have been written down instead.

Africa Fact

Africa's population is younger than anywhere else in the world. In Central and East Africa, around half the population is under 18 years of age.

Women in Africa

Most African societies are led by men, but women often have the most important roles in daily life. Women will often organize children in helping with tasks such as farming, cooking, shopping, and childcare. They will also cook the family meal and may earn an **income** by selling things or having a job. As more Africans move to cities and leave traditional societies behind, women are giving birth to fewer children.

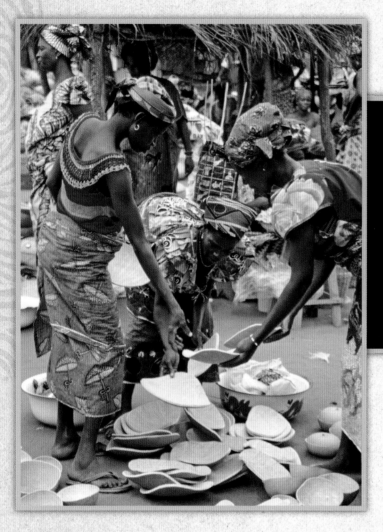

These women are discussing the price of bowls and plates in Togo. Markets like this can be found throughout Africa, and act as an important social centre.

AFRICA FACT

In some African societies, men have more than one wife. This is called polygamy. In polygamous families the first wife is normally in charge of the other wives.

African food

Food is important in African life and each region has its own specialities. Some of these have become famous outside of Africa, such as tagine (stew) from Morocco or biltong (dried meat) from South Africa. Lesser-known specialities include matoke from Uganda, which is a type of plantain (a fruit similar to banana) eaten with a rich groundnut (peanut) sauce. Food is often based on what is locally available, so seafood such as octopus stew is popular in the Cape Verde islands.

Hunger and diet

Not everyone in Africa has enough food to eat and many people go hungry. Another problem for Africa is that even when people have food, their diet can be very poor. They may eat only the same foods, like maize or millet (types of cereal), everyday. These foods are missing important **nutrients**, such as minerals and vitamins, which the body needs to stay fit and healthy.

Education

Fewer African children attend school than in most of the rest of the world. This is considered a major problem for the people of Africa, but just as important is the type of education people have. In many countries the education system was introduced by **colonial** powers and ignores local knowledge and values. Many educated Africans find that their qualifications are not suited to life in Africa.

Students at a secondary school in Kampala, Uganda. Like many African schools, it has only basic facilities and is overcrowded.

Basic needs

Poverty in Africa means that not everyone has food, water, **hygiene**, and housing. People who lack these things are more at risk of disease and illness. Education can play an important part in reducing risks by teaching people how to prepare food safely or how to make water safe for drinking. Art and drama are sometimes used to teach health messages to people who cannot read and write.

Young girls fetch water in Galufu, Malawi. Safe water sources such as this one dramatically improve the health of Africa's poorest people.

Killer diseases

Malaria is a disease that is spread by the bite of a mosquito. It is one of the biggest causes of death in Africa. About one million people die from malaria in Africa every year, and most of these deaths are among children under five years.

Another killer disease is **HIV/AIDS**. Africa has more people with HIV/AIDS than anywhere else in the world. In southern Africa the disease is so bad that many adults have died of the disease. The **economy** has suffered because many of those who have become ill or have died are workers. Some families are now made up of grandparents and children only – South Africa alone has over 1.4 million AIDS **orphans**.

Biography – Nkosi Johnson

Nkosi Johnson was born with the disease HIV/AIDS in 1989. As a boy he campaigned for better medical care and treatment for people living with HIV/AIDS. In July 2000, a year before he died, he made a famous speech at an international conference on the disease. He said:

"Care for us and accept us — we are all human beings. We are normal. We have hands. We have feet. We can walk, we can talk, we have needs just like everyone else — don't be afraid of us — we are all the same!"

The music of work

Many types of African singing come from work songs that help motivate workers. The songs often develop a rhythm for digging the soil or pulling in the fishing nets, for example. **Jazz**, **blues**, and **gospel** music were all influenced by African work songs that were brought to the Americas by African **slaves**.

Men work together to thresh grain in Ethiopia. Across Africa, activities are often performed in groups. Songs are also sung to keep a rhythm and motivate one another.

Children's play

In many African households, children are expected to help with chores such as cooking, cleaning, and childcare, but they still find time to play! Singing games and team games are popular and do not involve any special equipment. Toys in shops are too expensive for many children to afford, so children across Africa have become experts at making their own toys. They use local materials, including other people's waste, to make carts, spinning wheels, or balls. In Malawi, children make brightly coloured cars, bicycles, and trucks known as "Galimoto" from old wire and waste metal. Some of these toys are considered art pieces by tourists to Africa, who will buy them to take home as souvenirs.

Sport and leisure

Long-distance running is a global sport that is dominated by African runners. Men and women from Kenya and Ethiopia have been especially successful and hold most of the World and Olympic records (see the table below).

A boy in the Maluti mountains of Lesotho plays with a toy guitar made from local waste materials. Many African children have become skilled at turning waste products into toys.

Long distance runner	World records held
Haile Gebrselassie (Ethiopia; male runner)	10 km (6 miles) 20 km (12 miles) 20,000 metres (12 miles) Marathon One hour
Tegla Loroupe (Kenya; female runner)	20,000 metres (12 miles) 25,000 metres (16 miles) 30,000 metres (19 miles)

Football is more popular and widespread than running. Some of the world's most talented players are African, but they play mostly in European football clubs where they can earn more money. The Africa Cup of Nations is the region's most important football tournament and takes place every two years. Egypt won the tournament in 2008. The football World Cup will be held in South Africa in 2010.

Religion, beliefs, and customs

The beliefs and **customs** of African **culture** go back hundreds or even thousands of years, but day to day beliefs in most of Africa now follow major world religions (see the pie chart below). Traditional beliefs have not vanished, however – they are still followed in Angola, the Central African Republic, Madagascar, and Togo. In other countries, traditional beliefs often survive side-by-side with **mainstream** religions. This mixing of traditional and mainstream beliefs makes religion in Africa very complex.

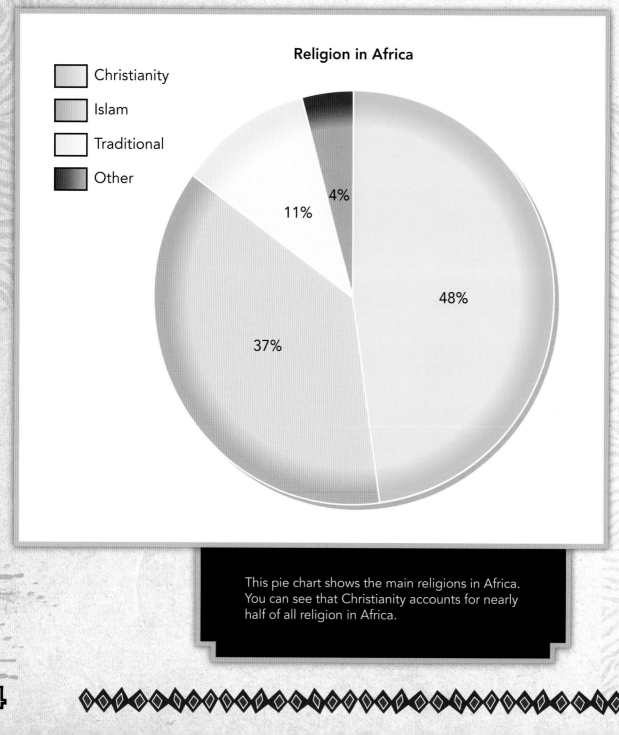

Religion in Africa

- Christianity
- Islam
- Traditional
- Other

4%

11%

48%

37%

This pie chart shows the main religions in Africa. You can see that Christianity accounts for nearly half of all religion in Africa.

Traditional religion

Traditional religions in Africa normally believe in a single "high" god with a number of less powerful deities. These are people or things (often on Earth) that are treated as though they were gods. Many religions also have animist beliefs where an animal, plant, or feature (such as a mountain) is believed to have a spirit or soul. **Ancestor** worship (the worship of dead relatives) is another important aspect of traditional religions. People will visit the **shrines** of their ancestors to make offerings or prayers during celebrations or in times of trouble.

Valuing local beliefs

In modern Africa, traditional beliefs are sometimes thought of as old-fashioned. Traditional medicine, for example, is often rejected for more modern health treatments. This is not true of all of Africa, however. In Uganda, traditional healers are registered with a national organization called the National Council of Traditional Healers and Herbalists Associations of Uganda (NACOTHA). NACOTHA promotes the positive use of traditional healing in modern Uganda. By registering healers it hopes to prevent crime by people who pretend to be healers in order to steal money from others.

A woman consults a Sangoma (traditional healer) at Lesedi Cultural Village in South Africa. The centre allows tourists to learn about African culture and helps to keep traditions alive.

The arrival of Christianity

Christianity is the main religion of nearly half the people in Africa. It follows the teachings of Jesus and is thought to have first arrived in Africa (in Egypt) in around 100 CE. This led to the founding of Africa's earliest churches – the Coptic Christian Church in Egypt and the Ethiopian Orthodox Church in Ethiopia. Both churches were established by around 400 CE, and still survive today with around 40 million followers between them. Today, most African Christians live in countries south of the Sahara Desert.

Members of the Ethiopian Orthodox Church celebrate Genna (Christmas) at Lalibela in Ethiopia.

THE ETHIOPIAN CALENDAR

Ethiopia uses a different calendar from the Gregorian calendar used by most of the world. It is based on the calendar of the Ethiopian Orthodox Church and has 13 months instead of 12. It is also 7 years and 8 months behind the Gregorian calendar. This means that in Ethiopia, they celebrated the first day of the new millennium (1 January 2000) on what was 11 September 2007 for most of the rest of the world!

Ethiopian month	Gregorian equivalent dates
Meskerem	11 September–10 October (year starts on 12 September during leap years)
Tikimt	11 October–9 November
Hidar	10 November–9 December
Tahsas	10 December–8 January
Tir	9 January–7 February
Yakatit	8 February–9 March
Magabit	10 March–8 April
Miyazya	9 April–8 May
Ginbot	9 May–7 June
Sene	8 June–7 July
Hamle	8 July–6 August
Nehasa	7 August–5 September
Pagumiene	6–10 September (year ends on 11 September during leap years)

Christian missions

Christianity spread across most of Africa following the arrival of Christians from Europe. They came as explorers and traders, and then later as **missionaries** and **colonial** settlers. Christian missionaries came to Africa to spread Christianity and to do what they believed was the work of God. They built schools and hospitals to provide for local people as well as building churches for worship. European and American Christian organizations are still active in Africa today and continue to run many schools and hospitals.

African Christianity

African Christianity has developed its own style by mixing local culture with mainstream beliefs. These tend to be lively churches that make use of Africa's long traditions of song and dance. African churches can be quite strict. Their leaders do not always agree with the more relaxed rules being introduced by some churches in Europe and America. Many disagree with giving women more power in the church, for example.

Islam

Islam is Africa's second largest religion and a little over a third of Africans are Muslims. Islam is the main religion of North Africa and also has large numbers of followers in West and East Africa.

Muslims believe in one God, Allah. They also worship the Prophet Muhammad, who lived from 570 to 632 CE. His teachings, written in the **Qur'an**, mention five pillars of Islam that all Muslims must perform during their lifetime. One of these is the "hajj". This is a pilgrimage (spiritual journey) to Mecca in Saudi Arabia, the holiest place in Islam. For many Africans this is an expensive and difficult journey. Poor systems of transport mean that many who would like to make the pilgrimage are unable to complete their journey.

The spread of Islam

Islam arrived in Africa with traders from the Middle East. They travelled across the Sahara Desert into North Africa, and across the Arabian Sea to East Africa. Many of these traders brought new knowledge with them from Islamic scholars. Islamic schools were set up to share this knowledge as well as the beliefs of Islam. Muslim schools, or madrassahs, where children learn the teachings of Islam, are still popular today.

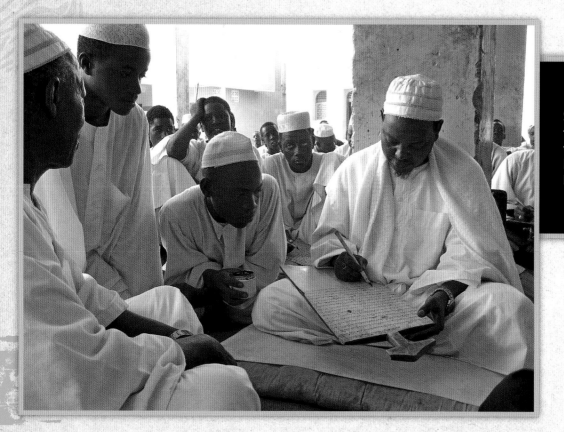

Students learn how to write verses of the Qur'an at an Islamic school near Khartoum, Sudan.

A man of the Sufi branch of Islam dances himself into a trance in Omdurman, Sudan. Those performing this dance are known as "whirling dervishes".

Islamic culture

Islam has a varied influence on the customs and lifestyles of Africans. Northern Nigeria, for example, has introduced strict Islamic law (Sharia), with severe punishments for those who fail to follow it. In South Africa, by comparison, Muslims enjoy much greater freedoms and mix their religion with other cultural influences.

In many parts of Africa, Muslim men and women wear traditional Islamic clothing. This is based on cool, full-length robes that cover much of the body. Women are often required to cover their heads with a hijab (headscarf) and their faces with a niqab (veil).

Performing arts

Africans use art in the way they dress, communicate, and share stories. Even household tools such as cooking pots are skilfully created to be beautiful as well as useful. Some forms of art are shared across much of Africa, such as a general skill in pottery or a love of dancing. Other art is more local and represents the **culture** of particular **ethnic groups**.

Miriam Makeba, or "Mama Afrika", was one of Africa's most famous singers and performed all over the world until her death in 2008.

African voices

Africans use their voices in a wide range of singing, and have a huge range of different notes and sounds. African voices are also used in storytelling, sometimes with music, to teach people about **morals** and history. Some of these stories have turned into well-known sayings or **proverbs**. Others have become songs that are now rehearsed and performed for pleasure as much as for their message.

Theatre

Drama and theatre in Africa started with people acting out traditional storytelling. Today, modern drama follows a similar pattern and is helping to keep many traditions alive.

The power of drama to tell stories and communicate with people is also being used to help with some of Africa's problems. Theatre groups have developed plays about the risk of **HIV/AIDS**, for example. They raise awareness of the disease by performing to schools and communities.

Dance

Dance in Africa is performed during celebrations and **rituals**, for healing, and for religious or spiritual **customs** such as those of the Sufi Muslims in Sudan and Egypt. The Sufi use a spinning dance to create a **trance** that they believe brings them closer to God (also see page 29).

Another style of dance is the jumping dance performed by Maasai men in East Africa. This is used to show their strength as **warriors** – the higher they jump, the stronger they are!

African music

Music plays an important role in African culture, but African music has also become famous and popular outside Africa. Celebrations and rituals almost always include music, and music is popular in the workplace, especially where a team of people are working together. Many traditional songs are types of farming song, such as the songs of Turkana men in northern Kenya which come from singing to their cattle.

Modern African music uses many traditional rhythms, instruments, and sounds, but often adds non-African influences to create new styles of music. This is sometimes known as fusion music because it is fusing different styles together.

URBAN ARTISTS

Positive Black Soul is a hip hop group based in Dakar, Senegal. They rap in English, French, and Wolof, a Senegalese language. They went on a 13-country tour called the "African Presidents tour" in 2005, and have also performed and recorded in Paris and New York. One of the members of the group, DJ Awadi, works with UN-HABITAT to help educate young people, and he also campaigns about issues across Africa.

African instruments

Africa has a range of musical instruments, but is best known for its skills in drum making. A drum is normally carved from wood with an animal skin (or sometimes a fish skin) stretched across it. They come in many different styles. The drum is played with either hands or sticks to create the rhythm for much African music.

Another common African instrument is the thumb piano, where different sized metal or bamboo keys are twanged with the thumb to produce notes.

Drumming is popular across much of Africa. These drummers are members of the Dogon ethnic group in Mali, West Africa.

AFRICA FACT

Because the sound of a drum carries further than a human voice, drums have long been used to send messages in Africa. They are particularly used by forest communities such as the pygmies of Central Africa.

Visual arts

African crafts use mainly local materials and so vary greatly across the **continent**. Among the most important materials are wood, stone, metals, and plants (especially grasses and seeds).

The weaving of natural grasses to make baskets is a craft found in many parts of Africa. These baskets are often simple and meet practical needs. In countries such as Uganda and Rwanda, the grasses are dyed in bright colours and used to create beautiful patterns.

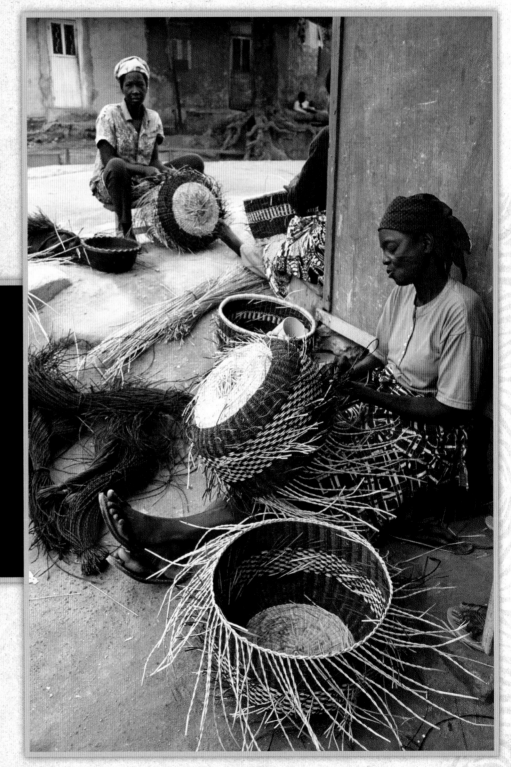

Batik

Batik is one of the most common types of **textile** art in Africa. It uses a combination of dyes to create designs for clothing or for pictures. A rice-paste or wax is used to prevent parts of the cloth being dyed. It is later removed to reveal the design. Some of the most complicated batiks can go through this process several times, each time with a different colour.

Art from waste

Africans have always been good at using what is around them in an artistic way. This tradition is continuing today with many artists finding interesting uses for waste. Paper is folded and rolled to make beaded jewellery, old tin cans are turned into lanterns, and old plastic bottles are used to make toy cars. This recycled art has become very popular with tourists.

The global crafts market

Some forms of African art have become very popular outside of Africa. This has created an industry producing African art just for **export**. However, some of the arts and crafts exported are not very genuine, and are based on what those buying them want to own. Some have said this is threatening local **culture** because skills are being used to produce African export art rather than preserve and develop local traditions.

AFRICA FACT

Art pieces made from ivory (elephant tusk) are very valuable. Half a million elephants were killed for their ivory in the 1980s. The ivory **trade** was banned in 1989, but an **illegal** trade in ivory continues to threaten the African elephant.

Body decoration

Celebrations and ceremonies often involve body decoration, but in some regions it is a feature of everyday life. In West Africa, decorative scarring is a common form of body art. Patterns are cut into the skin and then left to heal as a scar. In Ethiopia, Mursi and Surma women who are to be married have their lower lip cut in order to fit a lip plate. This is made from clay and inserted in the lower lip, which gradually stretches until it can take a plate of up to 20 centimetres (8 inches) across. Women take pride in making and decorating their own lip plates. Some other **ethnic groups** use similar techniques to stretch their ear lobes and wear an ear plug.

The Wodaabe of the Sahara Desert are one of many ethnic groups who use body art. Wodaabe men use make-up to enhance their faces and make themselves more attractive to women from other Wodaabe clans.

Africa Fact

The Fulani people of West Africa hold a male beauty contest called *gerewol*. Young men paint their bodies and decorate them with jewellery before being judged by the young women.

African jewellery

Jewellery is worn by both women and men in Africa. It is normally made using metals and beadwork (using wood, metal, or glass beads). The beadwork of the Samburu in East Africa and the Zulu in South Africa is highly detailed and uses tiny glass beads. Kazuri beads are sold to tourists and exported. Kazuri is a women's organization in Kenya that sells jewellery internationally and uses the money raised to help improve the lives of the women it works with.

Painting and modern art

Painting on **canvas** is relatively new to Africa, but some African painters now show their work in galleries around the world. Another common form of painting in Africa is on vehicles and buildings. This type of art is sometimes used for advertising things but can also be just for decoration.

Some artists use modern art to explore Africa's problems. The Nigerian artist Yinka Shonibare explores Africa's **colonial** past and its modern links with Europe. He has done this by creating life-sized models of European colonial scenes using bright African materials and colours.

Africa and global culture

As more Africans move to **urban** areas, they come into greater contact with **cultures** from elsewhere in Africa and around the world. This mixing of cultures is helping to create new urban cultures in Africa. It is also creating new audiences for African culture and making it easier to spread to other parts of the world.

Urban culture

Urban culture in Africa is based around television, music, and film. Music may be local, but it is also often the latest pop from Europe or hip hop music from the USA. Films and television programmes are also often from outside of Africa, since few African countries produce their own programmes.

South Africa, Egypt, and Nigeria do have television and film industries. Egypt is a major producer of films in Arabic, for example, and sells them throughout the Arab-speaking world. In 2006 the South African film *Tsotsi* won many international awards and created new interest in African film-making.

AFRICA FACT

A favourite TV programme in Uganda is *Hotsteps Dance*, a reality dance show similar to *Strictly Come Dancing*. The show has international dances such as Calypso, but also local Ugandan styles such as Bakisimba.

Writing Africa

African writing is one of the most influential forms of African culture. Novels and poetry by leading African authors have been read by people around the world.

- Wole Soyinka's plays, books, and poetry are often about the social and political problems of ordinary Nigerians. Soyinka was the first black African to receive the Nobel Prize for Literature in 1986.

- Chinua Achebe's most famous book is called *Things Fall Apart*. It describes the life of an Igbo community in Nigeria and how it was changed forever by European colonists.

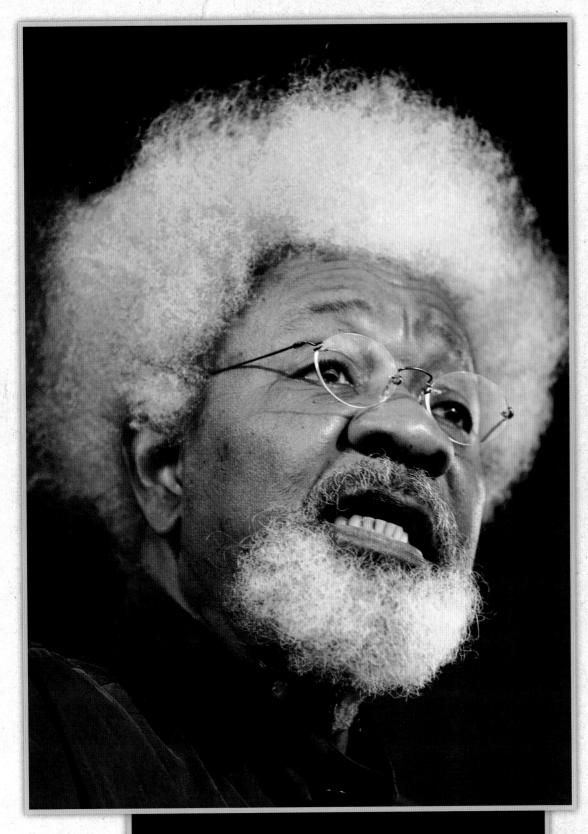

The Nigerian writer Wole Soyinka, speaking at a literature festival in the UK. Soyinka is one of Africa's most famous writers and is popular around the world.

New opportunities

New technology such as the Internet, email, and mobile phones is making it easier for African culture to be shared around the world. Mobile phones with cameras, for example, are allowing millions of Africans to take a photograph for the first time! The Internet allows Africans to share ideas with people on the other side of the world. The Internet is also allowing people to find out more about African culture or to plan a visit to discover for themselves.

African diaspora

Africans who live and work outside of Africa, or people descended from Africans, are known as the African **diaspora**. They are located throughout the world and many may never have been to Africa. Nevertheless, the African diaspora often feel close ties to Africa or to particular African countries. These ties are often maintained through cultural links such as dress, food, and music. The African diaspora has also played a major role in introducing elements of African culture to places outside of Africa. Shops selling many African foods, for example, are now common in cities such as London, New York, or Paris.

These Ghanaian women are taking part in a religious ceremony at a Church in South London. They are part of an African diaspora that today lives around the world, but still keeps close contact with Africa and maintains many African customs.

This rooster was made in South Africa from waste plastic. It is an example of modern African art. The chicken was a mascot for the rugby World Cup in France, in 2007.

African style

Like all places today, Africa is influenced by many global cultures. African culture is not being replaced, though. Instead, people have built on ideas from other cultures to come up with their own "African" alternatives. A good example of this is the popularity of Western-style clothing made with African colours and patterns that have strong links with traditional clothing. The Sakoba Dance Theatre Company from Nigeria mixes traditional Nigerian dances with styles from all over the world in order to promote greater global understanding between cultures.

African style is also influencing design. For example, furniture and **interior design** in Europe now uses many ideas that are based on African culture. There are even computer fonts that are based on African traditional culture.

Timeline

3100–1200 Ancient Egypt thrives as one of the world's first great **civilizations** on
BCE the banks of the River Nile in Egypt.

100 CE Christianity arrives in Egypt. By 400 the Coptic Church in Egypt and
Ethiopian Orthodox Church in Ethiopia are established.

c.700 **Islam** begins to spread rapidly into North Africa through **trade**
and conquest.

1415 The Portuguese create a trading post at Ceuta in North Africa. This
marks the beginning of European **colonial** interest in Africa.

c.1500 The transatlantic **slave** trade begins to develop, taking slaves from
West Africa to the Americas. Up to 27 million Africans are sold or die as
a result of slavery before it is abolished.

1807–1860 The transatlantic slave trade ends, after 400 years of slavery, and
around 12 million people being shipped from Africa to the Americas.

1833 Britain passes the Abolition Act to end slavery, and all slaves in the
British Empire are freed. Other nations follow Britain's example.

1865 Slavery ends in the USA at the end of the American Civil War.

1884–1885 At a Berlin conference, European nations who want Africa for its
resources and labour divide up the **continent** into colonies which
are ruled by them.

1948 South Africa's white government introduces a new political system
called **apartheid**, meaning "keep apart". It is designed to keep black
and white South Africans separate.

1950–70 More than 40 African countries gain independence, but colonialism
still affects people's daily lives.

1957 The first Africa Cup of Nations (football tournament) is held in Khartoum,
Sudan. Egypt wins.

1986	The Nigerian writer, Wole Soyinka, wins the Nobel Prize for Literature.
1987	The disease **HIV/AIDS** spreads across the continent. The southern African countries, such as South Africa, Botswana, and Swaziland, have high numbers living with HIV and dying of AIDS.
1989	A ban on trade in ivory is introduced to protect African elephant numbers.
1994	Apartheid ends in South Africa and Nelson Mandela is elected president.
1995	Over a third of Africans now live in urban areas.
2000	Nkosi Johnson, an 11-year-old South African boy, addresses an international conference on HIV/AIDS. Cameroon wins the Olympic soccer title.
2002	The Soweto Gospel Choir forms in South Africa.
2005	The Africa Remix **cultural** festival is held in London to celebrate African art.
2006	The South African film *Tsotsi* wins an Oscar for best foreign film.
2010	South Africa will become the first African country to host the football World Cup Finals.

Glossary

ancestor family member who has died. Some people pray to their ancestors for good fortune.

apartheid system of separation introduced by the white South African government in 1948. Non-white people were sent to separate schools, and even had separate seats in public spaces.

archaeologist person who studies the past by looking at monuments and artefacts from certain cultures

blues style of music developed by African Americans

bush land far away from where people live

canvas cloth used as a background for painting

civilization society with a high level of art, science, and government

clan large group of families who are related to each other

colonial act or process of making one country belong to another country

colonization taking control of a foreign country

continent one of the main areas of land on Earth. Many countries may be found in one continent.

crop plant grown for use by people, such as cereals or vegetables

culture actions and beliefs of a society

custom way of behaving in a certain situation

diaspora movement of people away from their country of origin, or a community made up of people who have left their homeland

economy system under which a country creates, sells, and buys products

ethnic group people who share culture and language

European Union (EU) group of 27 countries in Europe with close political, economic, legal, and social ties

export goods sold to another country; to sell to another country

gospel style of religious music developed by African Americans

harvest season when crops are gathered; to gather a crop

HIV/AIDS the disease AIDS is caused by the HIV virus. The virus attacks the body's ability to protect against infection. There is no cure for HIV or AIDS.

hygiene clean living conditions that prevent disease

illegal against the law

immigration movement of people into a country in order to live there

income money earned through work

interior design decorating a house or room

Islam religion based on the teachings of Prophet Muhammad

jazz style of music developed in the USA

language family languages that share some features

livestock animals kept for use or profit, such as farm animals

mainstream popular

missionary person sent overseas to spread their religion

morals how people decide what is good and what is bad behaviour

nomadic people who move from place to place to find food and water for themselves and their livestock

nutrient source of good health for the body

offering gift given during a religious ceremony

orphan child whose parents are both dead

plateau large, flat area of highland

proverb short statement of truth

Qur'an Islam's holy book, where the Prophet Muhammad's teachings are written down

ritual part of a religious ceremony which follows a set pattern

rural related to life in the countryside

shrine special place to worship

slave person who is forced to work for another

textile cloth or fabric

trade buy and sell goods

trance dream-like state

urban related to town or city life

urbanization process by which towns and cities grow and develop

warrior person engaged in a battle or fighting for a particular cause

Find out more

Books

Continents in Close-up: Africa, Malcolm Porter (Cherrytree Books, 2007)

Continents of the World: Africa, Rob Bowden (Hodder Wayland, 2007)

Regions of the World: Africa South of the Sahara, Rob Bowden (Heinemann Library, 2007)

Regions of the World: The Middle East and North Africa, Rob Bowden (Heinemann Library, 2007)

World Cultures: Living in the African Savannah, Nicola Barber (Raintree Publishers, 2008)

World of Music: Africa, Andrew Solway (Heinemann Library, 2008)

Websites

Africa Remix

www.africaremix.org.uk

Africa Remix was a 2005 exhibition at the Hayward Gallery in London, representing different kinds of artists from nearly every African country.

BBC World Service

www.bbc.co.uk/worldservice/africa/features/storyofafrica

This site explains the history of Africa and its people.

Kazuri Beads

www.kazuribeads.co.uk

This website will help you find out about this leading African jewellery supplier.

Soweto Gospel Choir

www.sowetogospelchoir.com

The Soweto **Gospel** Choir was formed to celebrate African gospel music, using talented singers from the churches in and around Soweto. You can learn the choir's song lyrics on this website, and find out where they are performing.

Places to visit

Many museums have good collections of African art and **culture**. Here are some of the more famous ones:

The British Museum
Great Russell Street
London
WC1B 3DG
Tel: +44 (0)20 7323 8299
www.britishmuseum.org

Pitt Rivers Museum
South Parks Road
Oxford
OX1 3PP
Tel: +44 (0)1865 270927
www.prm.ox.ac.uk

The Africa Centre
38 King Street
Covent Garden
London
WC2E 8IT
Tel: +44 (0)20 7836 1973
www.africacentre.org.uk

This is the main African cultural organization in Britain, but at the moment it is closed for redevelopment. However, the website does provide some information about African culture in Britain.

Index

Achebe, Chinua 38
African diaspora 40
ancestor worship 9, 25
ancient societies 6
Angola 24
animism 25
arts 30-37

basket-making 34
batik 35
Berbers 10
body decoration 36, 37
Botswana 6
Burundi 9

calendar, Ethiopian 26-27
Cape Verde 19
Central African Republic 24
children 21, 23
Christianity 26-27
clans 10, 12
clothing styles 9, 29, 41
colonialism 4, 12, 15, 19, 27, 37-38
crafts 34-37
cultural changes 4, 38
customs 8, 9, 10, 12, 24, 31

dance 31, 41
diseases 20, 21
Dogon 11, 33
drama and theatre 20, 31
drumming 32, 33

economy 21
education 19, 20, 28
Egypt 6, 23, 26, 38
Elders 12, 17
Ethiopia 22, 23, 26, 36
ethnic groups 10-12, 30, 36

family and daily life 16-21
farming 6, 8, 10, 18, 22
festivals 8, 11
first humans 6
food 19, 40

football 23
Fulani 37

games and toys 23, 35
Ghana 8

healers 9, 25
health 20-21, 25
HIV/AIDS 21, 31
hunting and gathering 6, 7

Internet 40
Islam 4, 28-29
ivory 35

jewellery 6, 35, 37
Johnson, Nkosi 21

Kalahari Desert 6
Kenya 6, 12, 23, 32, 37

languages 4, 10, 12, 14-15
Lesotho 23
literature 38
long-distance running 23

Maasai 12, 14, 17, 31
Madagascar 12, 24
Makeba, Miriam 30
malaria 21
Malawi 20, 23
Mali 11, 33
missionaries 15, 27
Morocco 19
music 22, 30, 31, 32-33, 38
musical instruments 6, 32-33

names 8-9
Namibia 6
naming ceremonies 8
Nigeria 8, 14, 29, 38
nomads 10, 12

painting 37
polygamy 18
population 17

Positive Black Soul 32
pottery 30
poverty 20
pygmies 33

rap 32
religions 11, 24-29
rituals 8, 31, 32
rock paintings 6
Rwanda 15, 34

Sahara Desert 6
San 6, 7, 14
Senegal 32
Shaka 12
Shonibare, Yinka 37
slavery 4, 22
South Africa 12, 19, 21, 23, 29, 38
Soyinka, Wole 38, 39
sport 23
storytelling 31
Sudan 28, 29
Sufi Muslims 29, 31

Tanzania 6, 12
technology 4, 40
textiles 35
Togo 24
towns and cities 16, 18
trade 4, 15, 28
Turkana 14, 32
TV and film industries 38

Uganda 10, 19, 25, 34, 38
urban culture 38
urbanization 16

warriors 12, 31
water sources 20
West Africa 36, 37
whirling dervishes 29, 31
Wodaabe 36
women 18, 27, 29, 36
work songs 22, 32

Zulu 12, 17, 37